MW01138832

The Asshole Whisperer

True stories about crappy leadership, jerks at work

and tips to deal with it.

Wendy Sellers,

MHR, MHA, SPHR, SHRM-SCP

The HR Lady ®

TABLE OF CONTENTS

DEDICATION

This book is dedicated to everyone who had or still has a crappy boss, jerk colleagues and/or asshole leaders in their work-life. You are on your own for your personal life.

ACKNOWLEDGMENTS

Thank you to all my friends, colleagues and strangers who shared their horror stories with me in the development of this book. I hope you have all escaped from those awful leaders and workplace environments. I also hope you spoke up on the way out the door (because you left, right?). On the other hand, if you figured out that <u>you</u> are part of the problem, I hope that you are attempting to see interpersonal situations from different perspectives. Why?

Because change starts with you.

INTRODUCTION

The purpose of this book is to help learn to deal with assholes to hold them accountable for their behavior, turn their behavior around or show them out the door.

Why I wrote this book:

1. Because there are plenty of jerks at work who are high performers, yet, no one wants to work with them because of their attitude and behavior. Allowing them to continue due to their technical performance affects the overall department or company performance because the non-jerks quit – or worse, they quit and stay.

2. Because I have seen too many employees do cartwheels down the aisle once a jerk at work (known as an "asshole" in this book) finally leaves the company.

3. Because people expect me to be my direct, blunt self in a book with a title just as direct and blunt.

What is an asshole whisperer and why do I want you to be *The Asshole Whisperer*? According to dictionary.com, a "whisperer" is a person skilled in taming or training a specified kind of animal, typically using body language and gentle vocal encouragement rather than physical contact. Therefore, in work life, *The Asshole Whisperer* will be one human taming another human or set of humans who exhibit a crappy attitude and shitty behavior regardless of their technical work performance. Oh, and apparently you can't just slap them (no physical contact, sigh). Can you imagine slapping your co-worker? Wait, you already have imagined this, haven't you? HR would be so pissed! Anyway, back to the advice. Why should you tame your coworker or a superior? It's because time spent at work is a huge part of our life and while it doesn't have to be all peaches and cream, it shouldn't suck. You need to make work less annoying for you and your coworkers by taming your coworker or superior. This also applies to any situation where several human beings must spend time together to accomplish a goal: a community project, the HOA, non-profit board volunteers, co-hosting events and so much more.

CHAPTER 1: Using Corporate Value Statements to Hold People Accountable for Their Shitty Behavior

My first book *"Suck It Up, Buttercup"* briefly delved into this topic. However, the goal now is to support you in developing value statements on your own so that you can understand why they are very crucial to removing assholes from your team permanently.

Once developed, company value statements should be included in job postings, job descriptions, team meetings, memos, email signatures, and every single performance or behavior conversation that occurs with an employee.

The first set of questions I urge you to ask is: are they really assholes, do they exhibit shitty behavior, and have they received crystal clear communication about the expectations of behavior in your workplace? The second question is: Whose responsibility is this? Yours or theirs? Hint: It is almost always yours no matter what your role is. As humans, not everyone "gets it" quickly. Communication (and often over-communication) is mandatory.

As discussed in *"Suck It Up, Buttercup"*, company values are a set of behaviors the company believes in and expects team members to uphold. They are sometimes called a moral compass and is often included in a set of ethics. If you are considering creating a set of values for your company, proceed with a deliberate action because every member of management must be guided by these values in their attitudes and behaviors in the workplace – from interviewing to the termination. This means that managers must be trained on how to hold people accountable via behavior management by monitoring and managing behaviors that violate your company values. To truly integrate the company values into your organization, you must plan so your employees will become engaged and your supervisors will not less stressed.

Let's **create value statements** or a set of company values in as quick as three one-hour workshop sessions. The more hands-off the executive leadership team is, the quicker the process goes. However, do not consider this a victory. Rushing through this process just to allow employees to be engaged and get a "win" may backfire down the road. Why? The company's values should be developed with long term intent such as the next ten years. If executive leadership is not truly involved upfront or does not thoughtfully review the proposed company values, they may unintentionally approve a set of values that do not accurately reflect the desired culture of the organization. This means that they will need to change the values in a short period (six months versus ten years). This sends confusing messages to the committee that developed the values. Plus, we all know that most people do not like change.

To get started, here is the process in 6 detailed steps:

1. Set up a diverse committee. This can be named the values committee or culture committee. However, you should only use the term "culture committee" if you are committed to these members long term. While the values might set up the company culture for success, culture is so much more than just company values. Culture is the personality of the company and that requires a great deal of commitment and authority. So, it is important to start with the "values committee".

Who do I choose as a member of the values committee? So glad you asked! Have 5 to 10% of your company represented (no more than 15 people) - for smaller companies you may need a larger number or in some cases the entire staff. You need seniors, baby boomers, generation x, y and z represented (and whatever is after z since we ran out of the alphabet); you need diverse gender/ gender identities; ages; races; sexual orientations; disabilities; and so on. Caution: do not choose your members based solely on their legal diversity. Are you confused? Don't be! Think about diversity and inclusivity as not just what someone looks like but also how they think. You want to make sure you have diverse departments represented; hourly and salaried employees; new employees and seasoned employees; a variety of education levels and work experiences including supervisors and managers; no executives. Get it? Good!

---

2. First committee meeting. Review company values concepts and the committee goals - and then give homework. Let the committee members know that this group and their decisions will affect the culture of the company for decades to come. Explain what the values will be used for (see hiring through firing on the next few pages). Depending on the current culture (ranging from amazing to toxic), you may need to assign homework and discuss in an open setting, ask for it to be sent in advance in email or even by an online survey with names withheld.

First, give them a homework assignment:

Part 1 - List 5 to10 words or phrases that you feel explains the company such as Integrity, Excellence, Growth, Fun, Family Feel, People before Profit, Innovation, Bottom Line, Profit, Success, Power, etc.

Part 2 – Research companies that you admire and find out what their company values/value statements are. Be prepared to discuss both at the second meeting.

3. Second committee meeting. Review homework assignments and discuss it politely; agree on the next steps, especially talking to co-workers and gathering feedback.

The more employees that know that their "friend" is on this committee, the more they will buy into the final values. Now, let's go back to talking it out respectfully. In some cases, you will have a loudmouth bully who can take over the meeting, talk over or at people and coerce people to agree with them. The best way to handle this is to set up rules *before* the committee starts meetings. Set up communication boundaries, especially if you know you have a member or two that will most likely stir things up. Don't go with your gut and not include them on the committee – as this is the best time to get their shitty behavior under control. Example: "Rules of Engagement for the Values Commitment: The Chair of Committee will act as the committee moderator in terms of communication flow, who has the stage and how long each member gets to speak". Speaking of the Committee Chair, you may also choose to select a chair, vice-chair, secretary, etc. You can do this by voting (in person, online, secret ballot, etc.) or by asking executive leadership to make the selections (this will depend on your current culture). End this meeting with a rough draft of the company values (words) or value statements (sentences or words with definitions).

4. Third committee meeting. The goal of this meeting is to agree upon the semifinal draft of the company values or value statements to give to executive leadership. Please note that this step may need to be repeated several times until leadership and the committee are aligned and agree to a final version of the values. Most of my clients can achieve this in three or four meetings. However, another client of mine with a set of well-established yet outdated company values took at least a dozen meetings over nine months.

5. Leadership approval and roll out. Once the values are approved, prepare to roll this out first to supervisors and managers (to prepare for training), then to the employees. You can do this by planning a branding unveil such as website updates, office posters, business cards, internal announcements and external announcements because it truly is a big deal. If you have a marketing team, get them involved. You will also need to hold customers to the values as well and be prepared to fire a customer for their shitty behavior.

---

6. Supervisor and manager training. At the same time as the roll-out or immediately before the rollout, conduct supervisor and manager training on how the new company values will affect all stages of the *employee lifecycle*: hiring, training, compensation and rewards, accountability and firing. This needs to be in-depth training so plan accordingly.

   i. Incorporate your newly created set of values and expected behaviors into the hiring process by adding the company values to all of your job descriptions and job ads. Create interview questions that will determine if the candidate truly aligns with your company values. Make sure you do not ask just "yes/ no" questions. Interview for attitude and behavior, not just technical skills and performance.

ii. Feature your values and expected behaviors in the training and development of employees by formally hosting ongoing workshops on soft skills related to your values (which often focus on communication, honesty, respect, trust, feedback, professionalism, etc.). You can hire The HR Lady ® to help with this (yes, that was a selfish plug).

iii. Blend your values and expected behaviors into your compensation and reward system by using a balanced scorecard (balancing performance and behavior). This will motivate employees to exhibit the desired values of the company to obtain more compensation and rewards while taming their shitty behavior. Additionally, create a reward program where supervisors and managers can reward employees who exhibit the values. This does not need to be expensive. This could be $5 gift cards for a fast food restaurant or a coffee shop, a $25 gift card for a home improvement store or a name in a lottery for a monthly drawing of $100 (taxable of course). I have several clients who have a funny prop in their office that they simply pass around when values are exhibited (ranging from a stuffed poop emoji pillow for dealing with crappy customers to a gold winner boxing belt for exceeding expectations). Start with a low budget so that employees do not expect something for displaying good behavior.

iv. Update your "performance reviews" by integrating your values and expected behaviors into how you hold the employees accountable. Change the title of your performance reviews to "performance and behavior reviews" or **"Accountability Reviews".** It is super easy. Just take your job description, which now includes the company values or set of expected behaviors and turn the job description into an "Accountability Review Form". Simply add a rating system to each bullet item on the job description.

Example:

- **(Performance)**: Analyzes logistics and organizes documentation

  Rating: Exceed, Meets or Below Expectations

- **(Behavior)**: Show integrity at all times

  Rating: Exceed, Meets or Below Expectations

v. Blend your values and expected behaviors into your termination decisions by firing based on crappy attitudes and shitty behaviors in the workplace.

Of course, by this time in the **behavior management** process, you have been documenting their bad attitude and behavior, have been very open with these jerk employees (who might also be supervisors, managers or leaders) and have warned them of the consequences of their bad attitude and behavior. So, this "you are fired" conversation should be a breeze. (Yes, sarcasm was totally intended here.)

Last but not least, create a feedback system, perhaps a yearly survey, anonymous or not, whereas employees can submit assessments of their supervisor regarding behavior in the workplace. Is the supervisor's behavior in line with the company values? Why do you need to know this? Who wants a crappy leader on their team? Not me! They cost you a lot of money and headaches. I do want to leave you a warning with this "360" review process so to speak. While you have already spent great deal of time training supervisor and managers on what the values you mean, you will probably not spend as much time with employees therefore be careful with jumping the gun and coming down too hard on supervisors due to vague or inconsistent employee feedback on supervisor conduct.

CHAPTER 2: Introvert, Extrovert or Ambivert? How Personality Traits Annoy the Hell Out of Others

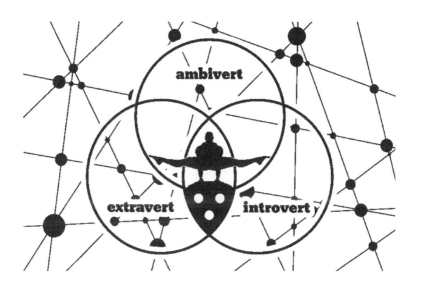

What the heck do I mean by personality traits? Traits are different from personality styles (such as DISC, Myers-Briggs and MBTI to name a few). Understanding personality traits will complement any knowledge you may already have on personality styles.

Our trusty friend dictionary.com states that:

- an **extrovert** is an outgoing, overtly expressive person

- an **introvert** is a shy, reticent person

- an **ambivert** is a person whose personality has a balance of extrovert and introvert features

Let's plunge deeper into these three personality traits. As you read through this chapter, be sure to note which personality trait you believe you are and which your colleagues might be – especially the colleagues that annoy the heck out of you. It might actually be you that needs to be tamed and not them. Guess what? We are usually part of the group dynamics problem. Be part of the solution.

Extrovert	Ambivert	Introvert
Naturally outgoing.	Outgoing when comfortable with it.	Naturally reserved.
Enjoys regularly spending time with people.	Enjoys spending time with others as well as time alone.	Enjoys alone time as a primary option.
Enjoys working on teams.	Enjoys working on a team well after working on individual tasks.	Enjoys working autonomously.
Enjoys talking through challenges and decisions with others.	Enjoys both managing information with others and on their own.	Enjoys working through details on their own.

There are also many very well thought out and researched scientific schools of thought regarding an "introverted extrovert" or an "extroverted introvert". This gets all too confusing for me, so I look at it in much simpler terms comparable to a scale. Generally speaking, people tend to consistently weigh in with one trait: extrovert, introvert or a mix of both (possibly leaning more one way or the other), the ambivert.

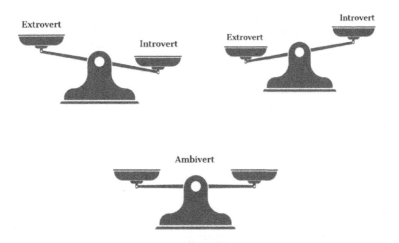

Lining your team members up with a job that matches their personality trait is vital for their success and the success of the department and company as a whole. A few job examples based on personality traits are listed below. Please note that these are not complete or scientific as a company must analyze every job based on the distinctive characteristics as well as each candidate's unique knowledge, skills, and abilities.

Extrovert	Ambivert	Introvert
Cosmetologist	Counselor/ Mediator	Accountant
Customer Service Representative	Paralegal	Editor
Event Planner	Police Detective	Graphic Designer
HR Manager	Registered Nurse	IT Manager
Physical Therapist	Sales Manager	Librarian
Public Relations	Teacher	Mechanic
Sales Representative	Team Lead	Researcher
School Administrator	Virtual Assistant	Software Engineer

Can you imagine relying on a solid introvert to conduct cold calls or attend a business networking event solo? Or requiring a solid extrovert to work at a desk on a data project, with no interaction with colleagues, for two days straight? An ambivert may also lean closer to introvert or extrovert, so pegging someone as "in the middle and fair game for all miscellaneous tasks" is also setting yourself up for failure.

Now knowing the basic differences between extrovert, ambivert, and introvert, ask yourself if your colleagues or employees are truly an annoying asshole or just different from you and others on the team? Whose responsibility is it to find solutions to work better with different personality traits and styles? Yours or theirs? Hint: Again, it is almost always yours no matter what your role is. Communication, empathy and educating yourself and others on your team is no longer optional. Refer to the charts in this chapter and make sure you have the right people in the roles designed to match their personality traits. I suggest going even a step further and educating the whole team on personality traits and why specific traits are needed for success in each role. Why? So, you and the entire team can **get shit done** instead of complaining about being annoyed by a colleague.

CHAPTER 3: The Other F Word: Giving *Feedback* Up and Down the Chain

By now (in theory), you have developed and implemented value statements in your workplace. The hard part is done - holding people accountable for their behavior is not easy! Performance is easy to talk about. Or is it?

Generally speaking, managers do a really bad job of telling people what we think about their performance and how they should do better. As managers, we get tied up in the "why" something didn't work when we should be focusing on the "what" - as in what do you actually want to happen?

"What" is much easier to explain and has concrete terms while the WHY could just be conceptual.

There are three business theories we accept as certainties: the theory of truth, learning, and excellence. The theory of truth essentially says that others are aware of your weaknesses even when you are not. Others know when your suit or dress doesn't look good and you rely on them to tell you. The theory of learning states that when you lack certain knowledge, skill or ability, you rely on those around you to teach them to you. And the theory of excellence is the belief that great performance is easy to spot and to describe and that once defined, anyone can improve their shortcomings with feedback from someone else.

In *"Nine Lies About Work"* (Harvard Business Review) we learned that these theories are false. **Feedback is unreliable.** It is based on what you, the rater, thinks are good or bad, positive or negative. And you might be an idiot. Your idea of dressing well might be awful, or you may not want to speak up to your friend. Your attempt at teaching others may be confusing or you may blabber on and make no sense. Your view of excellence may be unrealistic, or you may be using terms others do not understand. Of course, we also have these crystal-clear rating systems (sarcasm intended) that mean absolutely nothing and are a complete insult to both the manager and the employee. If you as a manager are intentionally rating someone average or poor and they are still employed on your team, guess what? You are an idiot! Why did you wait 12 months to tell them? Why are they still employed? Why are **you** still employed?

Managers believe that feedback has magical ingredients that accelerate growth. Well, no it doesn't. We all know that a Bloody Mary's magical ingredient is vodka - not pickled vegetables or even bacon. Although these items make the drink more enjoyable, without the vodka, you would simply be drinking tomato juice with vegetables and bacon. The magical ingredient for learning is not adding to something that isn't there. Learning is recognizing, reinforcing, refining what is already there. Therefore, feedback on what is already there is needed. For example, you can provide all the feedback you want on your employee's inability to speak French, but it won't change his or her ability or desire to speak French.

Criticism is not feedback. Criticism assumes your way is the better way and inhibits the brain from learning. Paying attention to weaknesses smothers the brain. Your brain responds to critical or negative feedback as a threat and narrows its activity. In a scientific study noted in *"Nine Lies About Work"* and *"The Feedback Fallacy" (both by Marcus Buckingham* and *Ashley Goodall, Harvard Business Review)* students hooked up to MRIs were asked what they were doing wrong and what needed to be fixed - their **sympathetic nervous** system lit up. The sympathetic nervous system prepares the body for intense physical activity and is often referred to as the fight-or-flight response. When students were asked about their dreams and how they might achieve them, their parasympathetic nervous system lit up. The **parasympathetic nervous system** has almost the exact opposite effect. This stimulates a sense of well-being, and even better immune system functioning. So, it's good for your health claims too! The study also argues that disturbing the PEA is critical when creating or affirming a personal vision. The PEA is an endogenous stimulant of the human brain that amplifies the activity of major neurotransmitters for multiple bodily reactions including a **sense of well-being** and higher performance of your body and brain. Again, all positives for your health insurance claims.

So now what? **Focus on positive outcomes and experiences.** Discuss scenarios or meetings that went well. Such as "here are three things that went really well." Tell your team - "let's do more of that! I want all of our meetings to look like that. That - yes, that!" Describe your experience when you catch them doing something good. Trust me, they already know how you felt when they screwed up. Say something like "that made me feel proud and excited." Managers (and non-manager too) quickly interrupt people to let them know they screwed up; how about you start interrupting them to say - you did that really well. Their understanding of what excellence looks like will be crystal clear.

Instead of saying "can I give you my feedback?" say "here is my reaction to what just happened." Or instead of "you need to be more responsive" ...try "when I don't hear from you, I worry we are not on the same page about the deadline." Or instead of "you lack strategy" ...try "I am struggling to understand your plan."

Throw in some positive emotion and compassion - change the game. Provide positive feedback that focuses on the strengths and abilities they already have or are capable of obtaining. I know some of you will have to dig really deep for this. (Hear me whisper 'you can do it, asshole'.)

If you are giving feedback up and down the chain until you are blue in the face and getting nowhere, **you might be part of the problem.** Whose responsibility is this? Yours or theirs? Hint: Again, it is almost always yours no matter what your role is. Communicating, empathizing and educating yourself and others on your team is no longer optional to get shit done. **Be part of the solution.**

As a manager, disciplining your direct reports is your job. Disciplining other managers' direct reports is not your job, but that does not mean that you should 'stay in your lane". Speak up respectfully and with the intent to truly help not simply bitch and complain.

If you truly have tried to give feedback up the chain, to your manager for example, and feel it is going nowhere, this is where courage, conviction and resolve come into play. Submit a calm, rationale, factual ~~complaint~~ *proposal of success* to your manager and his/ her manager. See how turning the terminology around into a positive is much more attractive to read and digest? No one wants to be attacked or critiqued. Your manager probably feels the same way. Tame your own behavior and pissed off attitude to be heard. If that still doesn't work and they make a decision that you simply cannot live with, then suck it up buttercup, it may be time for you to leave the department or company as a whole.

CHAPTER 4: Eight True Stories About Crappy Leadership and Tips from the Asshole Whisperer

This chapter contains true stories, anonymous of course, from submissions of a global online survey. I do not know who the participants were, and I am sure some of them are not going to be happy with my analysis and tips because looking in the mirror and accepting blame can sometimes be tough and that is exactly what I am asking a few to do. (Sorry, not sorry.)

True Story #1

First, he said to me: "I'd love to hire you for this position, but just between you and I, I can hire a woman for much less than I'd have to pay you." By the way, I'm a white male with several years of experience as a leader in a similar role. I was hired but not as the supervisor. Not too far down the road, he said "Let's not call it 'lying'" when I asked why they wanted me to be dishonest to a client's business partner/spouse. I was in shock over my boss's lack of integrity. The final straw was when I asked a question regarding the possibility of upward mobility and getting a higher pay rate since I came in underpaid and had been working very hard for quite some time. Then he said to me: "You see that guy over there?" He pointed to a much younger white male. "That's the future of our company. Your best bet is to learn the system and take all the projects you can."

At that moment, I knew I needed to find a new job as soon as possible. I felt completely disrespected and thought he was a real jerk.

The HR Lady's Reaction to the Story

My initial reaction was "wow, what an asshole that so-called leader is!" But then I thought, "well mister employee, he did give you key indicators in the interview that he was indeed an asshole." Always remember that an interview is a two-way street. Sure, the employer appears to have the upper hand but, in the end, especially during a tight market where it is very difficult to find and retain good workers, candidates have just as much upper hand (respectfully, of course).

Asshole Whisperer Tip

The Greek proverb states that the tiger cannot change its stripes and a leopard cannot change its spots. This means that one can't change their essential nature simply on a whim. It takes a long time for people to change, and it's only with dedication and motivation. So, give them motivation. Report unethical behavior, statements, and actions to the leadership team, owners or even the news if you must. Let's face it, you seriously do not want to work there anyway, even if you are feeling desperate, so why not fix the problem for everyone involved by standing up for the right thing. Respectfully report shitty behavior to anyone at the company who will listen or report it anonymously. Be part of the solution.

Waiting it out until you get fired may hurt your reputation and personal brand because they get to spin that story to fit their narrative. Yes, you may get to collect unemployment payments and/or a settlement payout (which is rare with companies that have crappy leadership) but when good people are always leaving a company, the word gets out and this affects their brand and reputation. Isn't that worth it?

True Story #2

My boss said to me "I know you're the expert, but when I disagree with your opinion, you just have to let it go." I felt like she did not trust or value me and that she was emotionally un-intelligent.

The HR Lady's Reaction to the Story

It's not a coincidence that "Let it go" is the signature song from the film Frozen. Be like Anna and do not let it go! My initial reaction is that this is not an effective management strategy. However, I am also only hearing one side of the story. What is the other side of the story? Did your boss mean: "Even when your expert opinion is the right thing for the business, it's more important for me to appear right than to trust you and do the right thing"? Or did she perhaps mean: "Yes your expert opinion on the data and research is completely accurate. However, there are other things to consider such as budget, timeline and as always, corporate politics."

Asshole Whisperer Tip

Break the damn icy spell of Frozen by gathering all the facts and then (and only then), by respectfully speaking up and offering multiple solutions. Consider that you might be part of the problem and instead be part of the solution. Here is what you can expect by asking more detailed questions to a comment like that from your boss: 'Wow, that worked' or 'well that's that, I quit'. Your boss is human too. Humans screw up. All the damn time! Simply ask her to clarify what she meant by letting it go and if she can help you understand it better than you currently do.

"Hi Karen (or whatever her name is), I realize you disagree with my opinion on the ABC project and I respect that. Is it because there is an issue with my research or is there something else that I am not aware of or even privy to? If it is something that cannot be discussed, I completely understand. I just want to provide you with the best solutions possible."

True Story #3

"It wasn't as much what she said, but how she said it. Nothing was good enough for her. There was no encouragement and no positive recognition. Perhaps she was trying to push me to work harder, but instead, I was always anxious and unsure around her. After a while, it was hard not to take her insensitivity personally. I became very confused about my marching orders, unmotivated, disrespected and, quite honestly, abused."

The HR Lady's Reaction to the Story

This one hit home hard for me. Why? Because I recall when I was the leader in this situation. I pushed a certain individual very hard to help him improve. Additionally, I withheld ongoing positive recognition because I personally didn't need it and thought it was only for weak people. Well, what an asshole I was in that situation. Guess what? I failed to achieve my mission – and he quit. I was gentle yet firm with his replacement and forced myself to schedule weekly meetings to provide simple feedback (what is going well, what is not going well, what can I help with). Wow! What a difference that made in productivity and the work environment itself.

Asshole Whisperer Tip

The tip to leaders is to find out how your employees want to communicate their marching orders and what motivates them. No matter what their values or personality traits are, everyone is motivated differently – on an individual level. You must get to know their motivations.

The tip to employees is similar. Provide communication options (weekly check-in, phone call, text, formal meeting) but make it intentional and as quick as possible. Not every meeting needs to be an hour. If you are only asking for 15 minutes every few days, your manager should be more than willing to grant that if it is purposeful. If that fails, move up the chain of command with your request. Afraid that will backfire? Doing nothing will cause you to be both miserable and ineffective, so pick your battle. If you choose to do nothing, kindly remove the words 'leader and trailblazer,' or 'does the right thing' from your resume regardless of what your ego believes.

True Story #4

"I worked for a private ambulance company which issued a memo from upper management stating in bold letters 'Opinions will no longer be tolerated'. It was, in their words, a morale-boosting effort and an attempt at humor." I felt disrespected and sorry for my new colleagues. I started looking for a new job elsewhere that day.

The HR Lady's Reaction to the Story

Sigh. Where to start with this one. My first question is: was the memo *really* from the entire upper management team or was it simply from one misguided individual who made it appear to be from the entire upper management team?

If truly from the entire upper management team, I am glad you started looking for a new job pronto because that is not the culture anyone should work in.

If you did some research, you might have found that it was from one person who may have got their ass handed to them after the memo went out. You would probably not know if this person was *ripped a new one* because the first rule of discipline is to keep it private. In this case, bravo to the company for handling the situation with as much poise as possible.

On the other hand, if the memo writer was protected by someone else in upper management (and you knew this for a fact, not a hunch – and know that I already question your facts), run for the door with your newly polished resume in your hand. If management truly supported this memo, it is a culture led by fear which is a huge concern as an ambulance company. Employees who are led by fear also tend to cover up mistakes and that is a huge safety concern for everyone involved – especially the warm body on a gurney.

Asshole Whisperer Tip

Instead of repeating "oy vey iz mir" which means "Oh, woe is me", verify the information before making a big deal out of someone's mistake or before putting in your notice. Once facts are verified and your gut instincts match the facts, take action. Nothing effects change more than high turnover and negative employment site reviews. Turnover often affects revenue and sometimes that is the only thing executives care about. And this is the whole truth.

True Story #5

"I was a department head who was grilled by my manager about an operational challenge in theme park operations. He called me at home and yelled (yes, yelled) at me (a grown adult) to the point that I was in tears. I feared future retaliation. My feeling is he was trying to shift blame to me due to neglect of his own duties while bullying me into fearing him. He said he did not want me to embarrass him in the future. All I could think is how did I embarrass you? I essentially performed your job for you. I felt he was an asshole. Not only did I feel abused, but I also was left feeling that he had mental health issues."

The HR Lady's Reaction to the Story

Any manager who literally yells at an employee is an asshole. The rest of the situation needs to be fact searched. A few questions I asked are: Was she doing his job? If so, what part of it? Was that actually part of her job and she didn't understand her job? None of that matters though as yelling at an employee can be considered bullying and intimidation as well as illegal discrimination. If the manager only is an aggressive asshole towards federally protected classes such as race, color, religion or creed, national origin or ancestry, sex, age, physical or mental disability or veteran status, then this may be illegal discrimination. Note that states, counties, cities, etc. may have additional protected classes.

Asshole Whisperer Tip

To the employee who felt bullied, officially report the colleague, supervisor, manager or leader to HR or a member of leadership. Make sure it is in writing and note the date, time and names of any witnesses.

To the asshole leader, please be a consistent asshole, regardless of the class of employees. You might get fired, but you won't get fired for discrimination. You can also try not being an asshole but to each is their own. Either way, here is what you can expect:

- Employees will quit - costing the company a loss in productivity and money to replace and train them.

- Employees will quit but stay - meaning they will not work hard or effectively as they used to while still taking a paycheck and using company benefits.

- Eventually, employees will file a lawsuit of discrimination for hostile workplace harassment.

True Story #6

"My former company, which gets a great deal of their funding from the government, sells a load of bullshit to their customers. Ironically, the customers are the taxpayers who fund the company. The company encouraged employees to oversell their service line to the customers. Everything was about quotas and not ever about meeting the customers' (taxpayers) needs. I felt like leadership as a whole was lying to the taxpayers and honestly, it made my skin crawl."

The HR Lady's Reaction to the Story

Without straight out saying I have been in this same spot (okay, I have been in the same spot), it is a very difficult, gut-wrenching place to be for anyone with a basic sense of ethics. The leaders - who are often the key stakeholders of the incoming revenue - often convince themselves that "what we are doing is ok" because we are employing people, providing benefits and helping the community overall. While this is true, it is only a half-truth. Taking tax money from the government for unnecessary expenses is not helping the community, the state or the country. Those funds could be used somewhere else – perhaps on homeless initiatives, assisting disabled veterans, feeding and educating the under-served, employing people who actually get shit done and so much more.

Asshole Whisperer Tip

First, as leaders, make sure you don't push your people to meet quota or goals that put your/ their ethics at risk. Closing deals should never comprise the employee's integrity. It is better to not make the sale or a project deadline than to have a customer buy something they either do not need or will not be satisfied with and therefore will complain about. In a private company, you can complain internally or even externally on employer review websites and/or quit. In a company receiving funds from federal contracts, you can go a step further and officially report it. The U.S. Government Accountability Office (GAO) is an independent, nonpartisan agency that works for Congress. If you suspect fraud, waste, abuse, or mismanagement of federal funds, FraudNet (operated by the GAO) can help report your allegations to the right people.

Whistleblowers can expect a shit storm to happen unless you can keep it under wraps of who reported it. As Shaggy sang on his 2000 studio album, "It Wasn't Me." Don't turn a blind eye or flat out lie to not get caught up in the situation. Don't be Shaggy, be *The Asshole Whisperer* by doing the right thing and reporting it internally first, then externally if you have to. Be the change you want to see. Be part of the solution.

True Story #7

"As a manager, I was told 'Don't ask employees if there is room for improvement or their opinions. We run our business the way we run it. End of story.' I'm not sure what my director was trying to convey. I was left puzzled and questioned why you would not want your business units or departments to run more efficiently or address issues that the employees are having? To me, my director's comment meant "we run our business how we want, and I don't want to hear how much we need to grow and change as a company". All I could think is wow what an asshole."

The HR Lady's Reaction to the Story

Well, he/she is an asshole. Is this a one-person anomaly or is the entire leadership team like this? It is important to know the answer here to take the proper action.

Asshole Whisperer Tip

Go above this manager and find out if the next level or levels feel the same way. If they do, leave immediately. If they don't, persuade them to allow for a confidential employee opinion survey for each department and the company as a whole. I do caution to not conduct an opinion (or satisfaction) survey unless a committee is both involved and prepared to take action on the survey results. Nothing can kill morale faster than asking employees for their opinions and then doing nothing about it. If that is the case, that asshole leader was right after all. In that case, run Forrest run.

True Story #8

"After 6 months of positive feedback and compliments regarding my work, my supervisor sent me a meeting invite 30 minutes before the meeting with the topic "6-month check-in". When I entered his office, he started the conversation by saying 'this conversation can go really, really bad or good depending on your reaction'. He then proceeded to say, 'this is my last-ditch effort'. I was thoroughly confused as to what this conversation was about because this wasn't a "6-month check-in". He closed by saying 'I need someone I can trust, and I can't trust you' with absolutely no justification for this comment. I eventually figured out that he was trying to communicate that he wanted me to be more supportive of his ideas publicly. Needless to say, I resigned a month later." My feelings were intense: I felt like he did not trust me and that he was just a crappy leader.

The HR Lady's Reaction to the Story

There are always two sides to every story (and sometimes three, four or more sides). Did this supervisor ever have any conversation with this employee regarding his desire for public support? Is that really what he wanted, or did he just want to appear to be on the same page? Did the employee misread previous conversations as 100% positive accolades and only hear what they wanted to hear? Did the supervisor ever put anything in writing?

Asshole Whisperer Tip

This mishap is 100% owned by the supervisor. If he meant "last-ditch effort", then he must have made an actual effort previously. I would like to see proof of those efforts. Remember that if it is not in writing, it didn't happen. Why? People forget things or don't take them seriously when not written down. If it was in writing, then the employee has to be held accountable and the supervisor needs to share the plan of action, timeline, and consequences. It is unfortunate that a possibly mix up of communication led to a loss of what I can only assume was a great employee. But kudos to that employee for having the courage to be valued somewhere else.

CHAPTER 5: More Stories About Jerks at Work and Tips from The Asshole Whisperer…to Get Shit Done

True Story #9

"My project lead said to me 'do you think you can handle the responsibilities of this project as a new mom?' He didn't want to tell me he posted the position internally already - I found out after this conversation. He was ultimately trying to dissuade me from wanting the role I had worked hard for over the past two years and which I was promised I would be getting before I was pregnant."

How to be *The Asshole Whisperer*

Well damn it, this is hot legal territory here. This is not just a decision that goes against company policy (and stupid) but seriously illegal on a federal level under the Pregnancy Discrimination Act (PDA). PDA applies to employers with 15 or more employees and is an amendment to Title VII of the Civil Rights Act of 1964. Discrimination based on pregnancy, childbirth, or related medical conditions constitutes unlawful sex discrimination under Title VII. I beg the question, **is there proof that you were promised the role before she was pregnant?** If there is, file a complaint then get back to work. We certainly don't want anyone to accuse you of trying to not put in the effort.

Company leaders need to get their heads out of their ass and train all supervisors, managers, project managers, and team leads about all employment-related laws, federal, state and local. Whether they are trained or not, the company is on the hook for discrimination even if it was unintentional. Having an HR department is not enough. HR doesn't have time to babysit your supervisors or put duct tape over their mouths.

True Story #10

"My colleague, who made a lot of money and had been with the company for 8 years, always said 'I just work here'. She expressed many times that she had no say about anything that happens here."

How to be *The Asshole Whisperer*

Point to the company Values and figure out a way to hold them accountable for their shitty behavior, even though you are not their supervisor. For example, a value might be listed simply as "going above and beyond".

"Hi Karen (or whatever his/ her name is), I wanted to chat with you about the statement you made when the team was discussing the XYZ project (whatever, whenever, wherever - be specific). I feel that saying "I just work here" is against our company value statement that everyone is expected to go above and beyond. I want to help our new employees feel motivated and productive by letting them know that their extra time and effort will make a difference. What are your thoughts on this?"

Please note that (1) stating "I feel" rather than "you are…" takes the blame off of her, therefore, this is important terminology to ease into the conversation; (2) expect this to go over like a lead balloon with most people; and (3) give yourself a goal to try three times (and document it) before heading up the chain and stirring shit up, respectively of course.

True Story #11

"My first job was at a big four firm, the project manager used to change my work papers to be incorrect. I don't know why he did it. I initially thought he was trying to help me. When the partner asked about the work product with errors, he would say 'I'm not sure, we have to ask her'. I would then say those aren't my words or my work, but he wouldn't own up to it. This happened several times to the point where I kept my original work to prove the significant changes. In the end, a partner told me he knew I was doing the work correctly, but I didn't get a raise or anything because of it nor did he get held accountable."

How to be *The Asshole Whisperer*

Is there an opportunity where you can provide feedback to leadership about this concern? The answer is always yes for this question. You may not want to do it, but the **opportunity** is always there. You can file an official complaint or drop off a covert anonymous packet. Just make sure your information is factual and not emotional. You don't want egg on your face!

Once you let someone get away with taking advantage of you, they know that you will not stir the pot and therefore they will continue to take advantage of you. Stir the damn pot (professionally and factually, of course).

True Story #12

"My shift leader told me 'I believe your coworker was sexually harassing you because you are flirtatious'. That bastard made me feel like the guilty party."

How to be *The Asshole Whisperer*

Is this behavior relatable? Yes, he is an asshole and it is undoubtedly against policy and the company values. Additionally, the shift leader and sexual harasser are both breaking federal law related to harassment and discrimination. File a complaint with HR and if that doesn't do anything, file a formal complaint with the Equal Employment Opportunity Commission. It is free. You do not need a lawyer; however, **you do need proof**. Please be careful if you are recording conversations without the other person being aware and know that this is often illegal. Check your state laws. It is better to have a witness's name, email, or text message.

True Story #13

"I was told by my colleague 'Your creativity scares people. You should dial it back in meetings.' I worked with lazy semi-retired people who didn't want to change and refused anything new. He was just as lazy so my pushing for change was an annoyance to him."

How to be *The Asshole Whisperer*

Sorry, but you might be the asshole here. There are a time and a place for brainstorming and creative solutions. The weekly staff meeting may not be the time or place. This meeting should be a quick run-down of who is doing what and who needs help so you can meet your deadlines, and everyone can get shit done. Sure, they might be lazy, or that might just be your ego-driven opinion because it has been made clear that you annoy the hell out of the team. Trust me when I say that they have their own opinion of you too.

But let's get back to your point. Do you want to be creative? Talk to your manager or find a job elsewhere. If you choose neither, then you only have one person to blame and that is you. *If you do nothing, expect zero changes.*

CHAPTER 6: In Summary, Don't Be an Asshole

Are you sick of people sugar coating how to deal with crappy leadership and jerks at work? Sometimes, people are jerks and you have to deal with them. Sometimes, you are the jerk! Jerks and assholes are everywhere. There is simply no escaping them. How you deal with them is up to you but avoiding them is simply not an option. Being an asshole to them isn't the best choice either.

Let's summarize my advice (if you choose to take it to tame these beasts). **First, create and stick to your**

corporate values or value statements; make it mandatory to hire with values in mind and to fire employees for violating them. It makes it easy to say, hey you're an asshole and I have proof.

Second, understand that people are different. Personality traits can't be changed so why don't you put people in the jobs that best fit their personality trait. C'mon, this doesn't take a genius to figure out, but it does take a little bit of time before you start the interviewing process. Get the job ad right!

Third, you have to provide feedback. "You're being an asshole" is fun to say but probably not the best advice in today's world (seriously, I wouldn't even say it at work). Plus, it isn't clear. Provide crystal clear feedback often and in writing – and then watch the magic happen as people suddenly understand your marching orders. Determine if the issues are performance-related, behavior-related, or a feedback related up. Also, ask yourself "Am I part of the problem? How can I be part of the solution?"

Finally, if you don't have the guts to hold yourself and other people accountable, **develop an asshole budget.** If you are a manager, leader or owner, your lawyer and recruiter are going to need a budget for the unavoidable consequences of asshole behavior. If you are an employee, you're going to need to save up income for when you are in between jobs every few months due to your asshole behavior. It is cheaper though to simply not be an asshole. Instead, be *The Asshole Whisperer.*

In the introduction, I told you there would be a test. I wasn't kidding. Grab a pen and flip to the next page. Receiving an "A" takes a lot of hard work, dedication, and self-reflection. Enjoy and good luck.

The Asshole Whisperer Test

A.   What are the top three ideas or solutions that you wrote down as takeaways?

1. _____

2. _____

3. _____

B.   What date do you intend to implement these by?

Date 1: _____

Date 2: _____

Date 3: _____

C.   Who will you ask to hold you accountable for getting this shit done?

Name 1: _____

Name 2: _____

Name 3: _____

D. What 3-5 values are important to you in a company or a boss? Write them here:

1. _____

2. _____

3. _____

4. _____

5. _____

E. Does your company/ department/ manager exhibit these?

<u>Yes or No</u>

If you selected Yes, congratulations. It is a rare find.

If you selected No, what do you plan on doing about this to be the change you want to see in your world?

1. _____

2. _____

3. _____

4. _____

5. _____

THANK YOU

"Thank You" to all the asshole leaders out there who inspired me to write this second book and fight for the managers and employees who you have walked on top of.

And a double "Thank You" to all the amazing people who have chosen to stand up and do the right thing for your company, colleagues, customers and the community in general by using self-education and the dedication to never, ever give up.

The definition of insanity is "doing the same thing over and over again and expecting a different result." Well, screw that! Be a disruptor. Be *"The Asshole Whisperer"* and get shit done.

Wendy Sellers,
The HR Lady®

get shit done

"You might be part of the problem. Be part of the solution."

ABOUT THE AUTHOR

Wendy Sellers, MHR, MHA, SHRM-SCP, SPHR has a master's degree in Human Resources, a master's degree in Health Care Administration. She is a passionate HR Consultant, Trainer, Advisor, Leadership Coach, and Speaker. She has worked with hundreds of corporations, small businesses, non-profits, and associations conducting management training, leadership development and HR advisory services leading to positive and productive corporate cultures. Wendy offers nationwide HR services for dirt cheap.

While she is not looking to make history, she desires to be the change she wants to see in this world. She says, "I speak up and challenge the status quo. I ask controversial questions. I correct facts".

She is both The HR Lady ® and The Asshole Whisperer.

www.thehrlady.com

Made in United States
North Haven, CT
05 September 2022

23621673R00050